Craft

Before You Start...

 The activities are designed for adults and children to do together. With a closet or a box full of craft supplies and a spare ten minutes, it's amazing what you can create!

 The activities should take about ten minutes once the materials have been assembled. Every child is different and often a project is worth continuing beyond the time limit.

 Step-by-step instructions are usually followed by examples showing how to extend the activities. If you don't have the exact materials, use anything suitable you have on hand.

 Warning: All steps involving scissors or sharp objects should be performed by adults, not children.

First Activities

Before trying anything more ambitious, help young children practice threading and pasting.

Put some tape around the end of some yarn and thread pasta onto it.

Make patterns using beads threaded onto pipe cleaners or string.

Paste things like buttons, pom-poms, or fabric onto pieces of paper.

2

In the Storage Closet

Make the most of your activity times by keeping a well-stocked craft closet.

Essentials

If you only have a few craft materials at home, these are the ones to collect: paint brushes, paints, colored markers and pencils, scissors, glue, tape, paper, and poster board.

Luxury Items

Glitter, feathers, pipe cleaners, and special types of paper are some of the many supplies that will add magic to your child's craft work.

Things to Collect

Recycle everyday items such as cardboard tubes, egg cartons, buttons, and yarn for all your craft activities.

Sewing Shapes

You will need: paper plate, paint, paint brush, needle, yarn, and colored markers.

1 Make twelve holes around the edge of a painted paper plate and twelve more opposite on the inner rim.

2 Thread a kid's needle through the holes and begin sewing as shown.

3 Sew in and out through the holes until the sun has all its rays. For older children, number the holes on the back of the plate, especially for more complex sewing patterns.

Give the sun a smiling face using colored markers

4

Bowling Pins

You will need: empty soda bottles, thick paint, paint brush, funnel, sand, and a ball.

Use several coats of paint if necessary

1 Soak the labels off six plastic bottles. Fill each bottle with some sand using a funnel. Replace each bottle cap.

2 Paint the bottles using thick paint. When they are dry, line them up and try to knock them down with a ball.

Add numbers and use them for scoring

Dinosaur Finger Puppets

You will need: felt, scissors, construction paper or craft foam, glue, and a button.

1 Cut out a dinosaur shape from paper or foam and make two finger holes.

2 Cut out enough small, square felt shapes to cover the dinosaur.

3 Glue the felt squares onto the dinosaur making sure that the base is covered.

4 Glue on a large button for the eye and add any other decorative details such as the ones shown on the opposite page.

Large button for the eye

Holes large enough for fingers to go through

Ptolemy Pterodactyl

Sponge green paint onto yellow poster board or craft foam to create this mottled effect.

Sequin eye

Finger holes

Tracy Triceratops

Glue a horned face onto a felt-covered base edged with bubble wrap.

Peter Parasaurolophus

Cover the dinosaur shape with glue. Sprinkle with silver and gold glitter.

Paint dabbed on with a sponge

Paper eyes

Felt nose

Finger holes

Finger holes

7

Papier-mâché Plates

You will need: newspaper, plate, petroleum jelly, flour, water, paint, paint brush, and decorations.

1 Tear up some strips of old newspaper. Cover a plate with a thin layer of petroleum jelly.

2 Layer strips of paper over the plate. Brush on a layer of paste made from one cup of flour and two cups of water mixed together. Repeat until there are four layers.

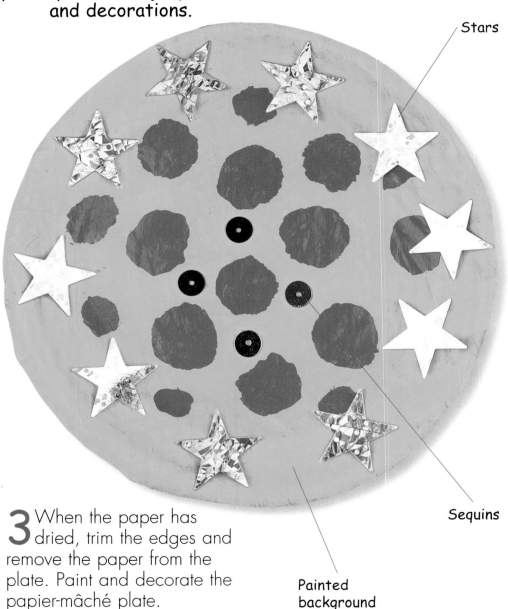

Stars

Sequins

Painted background

3 When the paper has dried, trim the edges and remove the paper from the plate. Paint and decorate the papier-mâché plate.

Face Plates
Use part of the untrimmed paper for hair and then paint on a face.

Fabric flower hair accessories!

Part of a bendy straw

Green painted cup and saucer with yellow spots

Play Cup
Make some papier-mâché using a cup with no handles. Add a layer of varnish or glaze if you have some.

Bright colorful paints make striking designs

Tea Party
Make your own tea set using different sized plates, cups, and saucers.

9

Fabulous Frames

You will need: poster board or paper, scissors, glue, fabric, tape, and a photograph.

1 Cut out a photo frame from poster board. Be sure the inner dimension is slightly smaller than your photograph.

2 Glue the frame onto the back side of a piece of fabric that is just a little bit larger than the frame.

3 Cut out the fabric at the center. Make a small cut in each corner. Glue down the edges onto the back.

4 Tape the photograph to the back. Add a piece of string or ribbon to one side if you want to hang the frame.

Choose a fabric that suits your photograph

Jellybeans
Put jellybeans onto a poster board frame using double-sided transparent tape.

Silver foil

Love Hearts
See if you can match the shape of the frame to the candies or to the photo!

It helps to use candy you don't like in order to end up with enough for the frames!

Candy Collage
Big, bold candy pieces make an effective but simple design.

Thick border for larger candy

Spooky Spider's Web

You will need: paper, colored pencil, glue, straws, yarn, pom-pom, and pipe cleaner.

1 Draw a spider's web onto some black paper using a white colored pencil.

2 Cut straws to fit on top of the white lines. Glue them into position.

3 Glue two circles of yarn to the straws. Finally, make the spider by gluing eight short pipe cleaner legs onto a fluffy pom-pom body.

Place the spider over the yarn as though it is weaving its web

12

Fun with Flowers

You will need: baking cups, paints, paint brush, beads, straw, scissors, fabric, and construction paper or craft foam.

1 Find three different sizes of baking cup. Paint their sides and centers.

2 Cut out two oval leaves from paper or craft foam and punch a hole in one end.

3 Use a bead to secure the leaves onto a bendy straw as shown above.

4 Make a hole in the center of the baking cups. Push the cups onto the straw and decorate the flower face.

Glitter gel flower face

Use beads or fabric shapes for the center

Painted pasta eyes

Tie the flowers together with ribbon

Music Makers

You will need: shoe box, scissors, foil, glue, stickers, glitter, cardboard tube, paint, paint brush, hair elastics, rubber bands, and a straw.

1 Cut a hole in the bottom of a shoe box, then cover the box with foil.

2 Decorate the box with glitter, stars, sequins, or stickers.

3 Paint a long cardboard tube. Put the hair elastics or rubber bands on as guitar frets.

Plastic straw bridge

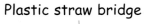

4 Glue a straw to the left-hand side of the hole, then stretch four rubber bands over the box. Lastly, glue the tube to the box.

Rubber band strings

Hair elastic frets

Soda Bottle Shaker

Fill an empty soda bottle with hard, dried food such as lentils, pasta, or rice. Tape strips of paper that rustle to the end, then shake the bottle!

Rustling strips of foil and paper

Pasta, rice, barley, lentils, or popcorn

Band of card to cover the ends of the paper strips

Jam Jar Xylophone

Fill some jars with different amounts of water and add some food coloring to each one. Test the sounds that the jars make by tapping each jar on its side.

Use a paint brush or pencil to tap the jars

Sticky Pictures

You will need: paper, scissors, glue, foil, magazines, tissue paper, and marker pens.

1 Cut out a fish shape from construction paper.

Black eye, mouth, and gill

2 Glue circles cut from foil and old magazines to both sides of the fish. Put the foil ones at the top and the others at the bottom.

3 Draw in eyes, mouth, and gills. Glue strips of tissue paper to the tail. Suspend the fish from the ceiling.

16

Jolly Jellyfish

Glue tissue paper circles to the jellyfish's body. Then attach long strands of colored yarn for the tentacles.

Long lengths of colored yarn

5, 4, 3, 2, 1...

Cut a rocket ship out of black paper. Cover with white paper rectangles. Glue red and yellow paper flames to the bottom, then glue everything onto a large piece of fiber fill or cotton.

Black paper rocket shape

White tiles

Fiber fill or cotton glued to a black paper background

17

Picnic Train

You will need: small cereal box, matchbox, juice carton, paper, scissors, glue, construction paper, foil, paint, paint brush, and a pipe cleaner.

Push the straw into the juice carton

1 Cover the boxes with colored paper including the unopened juice.

2 Cover six construction paper circles with foil to make the wheels.

4 Attach a pipe cleaner hook to the matchbox draw and fill the train with picnic goodies.

3 Glue the boxes together as shown with three wheels on each side. Add black paper windows and give the train a number.

Pipe cleaner hook to open the secret drawer

Container Ship

You will need: cereal box, scissors, stapler, paper, cardboard tubes, paint, and glue.

1 Cut out this shape using the bottom and two sides of a cereal box. Then cover it with blue and white paper.

2 Bring the two sides of the ship shape together and staple them at the top.

3 Paint one tube red, one yellow, and cover the last one with silver paper.

Colored markers

Paint brushes and scissors

Colored pencils

4 Slip the tubes inside the ship and glue on four paper port holes to each side. Use the tubes to store pens, pencils, and brushes.

White paper port holes

19

Bat Mask

You will need: egg carton, paint, paint brush, scissors, felt, stick, poster board, and glue.

1 Cut out the carton as shown and make two holes in the base.

2 Paint the outsides using orange and black paint.

3 Cut out the shape of a bat's head and wings from gray felt. Glue the felt onto some poster board cut to the same shape.

Gray felt bat shape glued to poster board

Silver stick for holding the bat mask

4 Push a silver painted stick through one side of the egg carton eyes. Then glue the eyes to the felt outline to complete the bat mask.

Crazy Caterpillar

You will need: long egg carton, paint, paint brush, pipe cleaners, scissors, paper, beads, cotton balls, sprout seeds, and water.

1 Cut an egg carton in half lengthwise. Trim the sides to make them even. Paint the carton orange.

2 Glue on pipe cleaner legs. Fill the egg spaces with cotton balls. Sprinkle seeds onto the cotton balls, water gently, and cover with paper until they sprout.

3 Make a face for the caterpillar and glue it to the body. The seeds should take about a week to grow. Make sure they are watered daily.

Pipe cleaner feelers

Sprouts ready for cutting

Yellow paper caterpillar face

Pipe cleaner legs

Hats and Masks

You will need: poster board, tape, glue, glitter, stickers, tissue paper, stapler, felt, pom-pom, stick, scissors, foil, fabric, and feathers.

Princess Hat

1 Roll some poster board or construction paper into a cone. Tape the sides together.

2 Decorate the cone with glitter and make a border out of colored stickers.

3 Tape some tissue or crepe paper to the top and then glue on a sparkly pom-pom.

Yankee Doodle Hat

1 Make a tube shape using poster board. Cut the top of the tube at an angle.

2 Cut out a felt circle to fit around the base of the poster board hat.

3 Staple the felt to the tube. Push a feather in the hat and call it macaroni!

Love Heart Mask

1 Cut out two felt hearts. Glue them onto poster board or construction paper cut to the same shape. Make two eye holes.

2 Glue the hearts together. Add a glitter border and glue a stick covered with foil to one side.

Red head feathers

Mysterious Bird Mask

Use some furry fabric glued to poster board or construction paper. Tie some elastic to holes in the sides or glue the mask to a stick.

Furry black fabric

Yellow paper beak

Kids' Gallery

With thanks to all the children who helped us make this book.

Fairy Plate by Kelly

Candy Frame by Conor

Super Rocket
by Harry

Flying Fish by Natasha